# Man Afield

by

Jim Krosschell

Prolific Pulse Press LLC, Publisher
Published March 2026
Raleigh, North Carolina USA



Permission requests are to be directed to:
Admin@prolificpulse.com

ISBN 978-1-962374-79-8 Paperback
ISBN 978-1-962374-80-4 ePub

Library of Congress Control Number: 2026904795

To Cindy, Kate, and Emma

# Contents

# Proem

## Multitudes

A population of more than a hundred ducks swims
in the cove today, along with, improbably, some
hundred white gulls. Several times all rise and
swirl and quickly turn back, contradicting
themselves in response to a stimulus
unknown to amateur scientists
or even to such poets who
would like to contain
birds and every
other living
thing in
words
like
I

# On Deck

**Bird Baiting**

It doesn't really hum, more a buzz,
it cannot be a bird, more like a bee,

mis-named impossibility, then, this
jewel flying backwards that startles

me each time it bombs the red glass
flower, and then stops, hovers, sips

liquid donuts from plastic petals, all
of which I've furnished so I can be

interrupted from ennui and reverie
and hijack its wildly beating heart.

**Ants on a Table**

### Work
The very definition of industry,
you careen around this blank,
glass-topped table,
following a way I don't see.
Lao Tzu says, "An ant on the move does more than a dozing ox."

### Play
Some of you can run 100 body lengths per second;
that's like me running 300 miles per hour.
There are three of you to an inch;
I am 200 times bigger.
You dashing around the tabletop
is like me skating on a ten-acre rink.
Apparently, you like the simplicity
of smooth, slick surfaces.
Apparently, you score goals with quantum pucks.

### Eat
You drag around the carcass of a fly
bigger than you.
How will you get home from this height?

### Believe
The paperback cover of the Tao Te Ching
lifts in the breeze.
You crawl under
to rest in the nothingness.

### Fall
In the course of exploring the side of the table,
you fall off a 600-foot cliff to the bricks below.
Stunned only for a second,
you resume your career,
but soon you go bonkers -
scurry - rest - scud - rest - scramble - rest -
until you find the nest
under the pot of impatiens and creep in,
to die and be recycled.

Sleep

I doze, wake, contemplate
a speck of dirt on the arm of the chair,
which moves and becomes
two gnats fucking.

## His Eye

A sparrow pokes at feeder seed,
lands on the railing of the deck,
and looks around this universe.

It graces me with glances, or so
I think. I can't perceive how I
appear in such partitioned eyes.

Where next? How does it decide?
Ah, simply to be ruled by hunger,
fear, maybe even chaos theory....

I know I'm not a saving choice.
One gesture, it's gone. God's eye
is on the sparrow, blinded to me.

**Wayfaring Stranger**

What did it think it was doing
as it struggled through forests of follicles,
marking a way for penitents,
or blazing a steep way home?

It scrambled from wrist into elbow,
and then a thumb came down hard
and broke its poor black back.

Arm, thumb were mine.
For a moment I was an Almighty.

# Three Minutes with a Chickadee

It lands on the arm of a chair
four feet away
and with bright eyes and quick twitches
surveys its world, including me.
It opens its mouth as if to warn,
but nothing I can hear
comes out.

It flits to the feeder
and makes its usual mess of the seeds
selecting only those of the sun.
On the ground below
the ordinary folks
like chipmunks and sparrows
forage.

It flies to the nearby rhododendron
perhaps to cache a seed for winter
and then up to an ash
to peck for dessert - bud, bark, bug.
I lose it in the leaves
until it circles back
again.

**Mites**

I'm sitting outside pretending to think,
or worse, pretending to write.
A sky of infinite blue,
and rich green trees etched against it,
are alluring distractions,
but I've become fixated (eagerly)
on tiny red spidery dots circling furiously
on the arms of the chair.

I touch one.
It squashes into a bloody period.

And then my phone importunes, reporting
it's not blood, it's pigment,
and they're not spiders, they're mites,
of which fifty thousand species are catalogued
and perhaps a million more still at large.

And so, like a poor widow,
I offer two mites to the treasury.
It's what livelihood I have.

**On Deck**

Plant litter -
                              pine pollen
             scraggly clumps of birch seeds
                   ash leaves prematurely yellowed

Animal litter -
        bird dung
                              a beetle on its back
               the carcass of a caterpillar

People litter -
             chair     planter
        table                        grill
                   flakes of peeling paint
                         rust

What's next to decompose -

Me - except I'm saved

                     by a perfect
                 green, half-sphere
               of moss, begot and grown
             on asphalt (!) shingles, set sail by
           wind and rain, fallen near my chaise,
        under a bright blue ageless orb of summer.

**Keep It Simple**

Carry out the summer chairs.
Sweep the deck of winter's trash.
Early April, come what may,
Easter's just another day.

**He and She**

She was having lunch.
He hung nearby, moved in.
Irritable, pregnant, she rushed at him,
wouldn't spare a bite, certainly not a kiss.
Woke, sensitive, he accepted his fate.
They retreated to their stations,
and nothing happened for the rest of the day.

Was this a stand-off in Schenectady?
Detente in Detroit?

Nah. Bored, needing my tropes to act,
I anthropomorphized
two brown spiders hanging
between screen and glass.
It didn't help.
Nothing continues to happen this morning.

But last night surely something exciting
went on while I slept -
repairing the web,
rutting like bunnies,
birthing some babies,
sharing the guts of the fly -
when I was alive to their world.

**Five Movements**

A silvery plane,
contrail dissolving, drops down
its unseen poisons.

White gauzy curtains
whirl like dervishes in wind:
fractals in chaos.

Green leaves etch into
blue sky. Neck cricks from staring
lately too much up.

Masking the buzz from
Route 1, bumble bees drone in
the rhododendron.

Oak leaves waft, ash leaves
spiral. Caught in flight I put
down my mind and watch.

**Overnight Success**

As tiny as a seed of wheat,
it must have launched itself
into the abyss
between my chair and the railing of the deck,
ropes trailing
(like me jumping off
the far tower of the Golden Gate Bridge
and swooping all the way to Marin),
and then it rests all day
on the slightest of gossamer threads,
every breeze rattling it like a hurricane.

In the morning, I see it's completed the web -
anchored in seven places,
artful concentric circles of death
(how easy it is to make something perfect)
and by noon its reward is a gnat.

Oh, spin me too an airship of silk,
let the wind blow me far.
Fasten me onto a headland of grit,
let the work of making a poem begin.

Yet

no matter how hard
a human can work,
concocting corrections late into night,
poems will never be perfect.

We send them out anyway, don't we.

# Yard Control

## Wolves

They roam the shoulders of I-95,
free runners of June.
We capture some in our yards,
we pen them in small preserves,
and they, like all beasts in thrall,
are desperate to keep wild things wild,
sending out seeds and underground stems
as if to civilize a ruined world
by covering it with baby wolf plants - lupines,
as they are known to humans,
as in, of course we needed to name them something,
as in, seeds, poisonous, that if improperly prepared for eating
could kill -
these fierce babies growing up
into the most beautiful of invaders,
until we, with our different view
of civilization,
rev a motor and mow them down.

## Red or Blue

How satisfying he finds it
to beat his head against the wall.
With what hormones springtime rages.
His territory threatened,
his nest and eggs at stake,
and a girl nearby cheering him on,
this warrior, birdbrain,
attacks, attacks again,
tooth and nail.
Or should I say
bill and claw,
for the other guy, his enemy,
is merely his reflection in the window glass.

Note that the red bird's own worst enemy
may be himself.
It doesn't seem to matter.
He loses brain cells, sure,
but proud boy gets the girl, controls the yard,
perpetuates the species.

While blue bird, also on the wing,
looping in what looks like happiness
across the meadow
isn't quite so brave.
He knows his enemies:
if a starling, sparrow,
or angry crow barges in
to take his house,
he'll fight a bit.

But being small and nice and pretty,
he tends to lose.
Ruffling his feathers,
complaining about the state of the world,
he flies away hoping for another.

# I Feed the World

The feeders now are so devised
that I can view them from my chairs,
both the writer's one inside
and the lounger on the deck.

Several hang from shepherd's hooks
to fuel the smaller passerines —
sparrows, titmice, goldfinches —
who seem to follow decorous rules.

The bigger birds cannot alight,
so bluejays squawk, woodpeckers dive,
phoebes perch, and mourning doves
(a threesome!) scrabble in the grass.

My smallest friends the hummingbirds
are more aggressive, warring round
the red glass cylinder, surpris-
ing me with nature's truculence.

But then the mammals - squirrels red
and gray, the cute brown chipmunks - come
to feed. I jump up from my chair
and make an angry, hissing noise.

My carefully constructed world
of supermarket nuts and seed
succumbs to what appears to be…
greed, although of course it isn't.

Still, it seems that birds are more
attractive since they're less like us.
Some days I wouldn't mind at all
if chickadees defined my world.

**Flying Ant Day**

On a warm and humid late August day,
the ants arose from nests in the yard,
flying up and out.
Squirt-sized males with torpedoes for dicks
sought mid-air coitus
with two-inch virgin queens,
for new colonies must be formed.
Terns suddenly appeared over the bay
(where have they been all year?)
and gulped ants down by the hundreds.

The ants also rose up from a nest
in the crawl space under the house,
and slithered inside through cracks
in the fireplace bricks.
They crowded the windows, floor to ceiling,
mistaking glass for sex.
Our daughters cried, "Eww!"
and ran out the door,
and I wielded the vacuum
and gulped ants down by the hundreds.

We still miss that house:
the excitement of two-week vacations,
wilder sex on surf-tossed nights,
walking with daughters on granite ledges,
and while this new house
farther up the bay
is fine for just two of us,
the quietude almost making up
for loss of surf and shelf,
when the terns fly in today,
uttering little squeaks as if even perfect flyers
somehow aren't well-enough oiled,
there seem to be only a few flying ants anymore.

I lean way back in my deck chair
and watch flights
methodically criss-cross the sky,
and when I'm called in for dinner.
I get up, well-oiled by multiple drinks,
but still slightly creaking.

**Sounds in a Hammock**


Birds - known, unknown - calling.
A red squirrel chattering.
Small waves slapping stones on the shore.
Wind frisking the autumn oaks.
Acorns ripping through papery leaves.

Dogs barking, for any number of reasons.
Children yelling and screaming, three lots down.
Leaf blower.
More machines, though faint and far away:
    trucks on the highway
    boats on the bay
    airplane high above.

Tinnitus.
Growling stomach.
Nylon netting squeaking when I clamber out.
Gunfire from Outdoor Sportsman over the ridge.
"All Things Considered"
tolling from the house.

**Naming**

When I walk around in my life,
happy and curious,
and a bright banded thing-in-itself
zips into view,
I at once want to look up
its name, its habits, its range,
in order to stuff it, I guess,
into a thesaurus,
so it will sit pretty on a page
later.

But there's danger here.

If I don't also
unname the creature
and lose myself
in the wonder of flight,
if I don't dance on the head of an anther,
stroll into the sweet Tao warmth
of a beehive buzzing,
then that thing will not
rise out of itself
to join all others....
And when I walk in the colony of humans,
it might be yet worse,
for the friends I make
and the stories I tell
could become mere fanciful facts
on the page,
or in the ear,
lacking wings.

**Yard Control**

In October two pots of russet mums replace
the scores of whirligigs and grinning gnomes
now stored in several sheds around the yard.
Each week the hunched-up woman mows the lawn,
and when the brisk wind litters it with leaves,
the old man blows them into darkened woods
beyond the crooked, two-rail, flimsy fence
that keeps out nothing.

Afternoons, on a rickety deck attached
to the trailer, in a patch of sun grown smaller
day by day, they drink from mugs and smoke.
Walking by and waving, I think about the deer
that nipped their plastic peonies last month,
and the turkey flock that disobeyed the sign
"No Trespassing."
Are we exceptions to the fearful wildness
to be kept at bay?

## Sitting Still

Recently, in a featureless room,
social psychologists conducted
experiments on attention span.
Most people, they found, would
rather get a mild electric shock
than sit for fifteen minutes doing
nothing. The supposition is that
we crave continuous stimulation,
i.e., can't abide our inner selves.

Now, repeat the experiment outside
on a warm September afternoon:
breezes brushing your skin,
a chipmunk nibbling the cupule off an acorn,
iced tea gladdening your throat,
the pine trees redolent,
a blue jay squawking in the hemlock,
and love-feasts from past and future
flowing through your head....

If you still can't sit still after that,
the shock you need may last
a little longer.

**How to Fall**

I'm suspended by hammock
between heaven and earth,
while the oak leaves fall
in astonishing geometries.
They
      spiral
         swoop
            twist
               plunk
                  ratchet
                     dive
                       waft

So many elegant ways to decompose.

And when these acrobats -
future worms, birds, angels -
land on me,
stuck in lumpish human land,
I help them
to the waiting ground.

## Cabbage White

The wind is quite substantial, blows the pages
of this devastating Trethewey
unless I hold them tightly.

The cabbage white flies helplessly against it,
fluttering jaggedly, dancing the
tarantella against it.

She's palpably insubstantial, a tiny
dram of drunken notes that flare across
the seeds and mulch of April.

Yet: symbol of peace, purity, luck, rebirth;
indomitable, stirred up, testing
the blank air like a poet.

# Standing in Woods

## White Man's Footstep

It arrived in the baggage
of the Puritans,
and spread as they did.
Wherever they dug a road
or slashed a wood,
there it grew, weedy.
But Maliseet and Cree
learned to eat its leaves,
to apply them as a salve
to wounds they suffered.
*Plantago major*
became a useful citizen,
naturalized to the New World,
unlike those who brought it in.

**Turkeys**

Seen on video:
two males strut up to a female,
gobbling, displaying.
Their snoods are engorged.
Muzak plays.

One of them twists violently,
drops.
The other one flees,
warily returns to nuzzle his brother's body,
even jumping on it
as if to say, "Quit playing around."
Then it too drops dead.

I now see
that the female is a decoy,
and the hero of the scene,
a young man wearing camouflage like feathers,
holds up his prey by the feet
and grins into the camera.
"I have never in my life
shot a turkey
in the head
with a bow...
and this guy came back
and I freakin' got him too."

He "got" him from ten feet away,
the same distance from my deck
where our local flock,
confident in human exurbs,
poked in the yard
earlier this morning,
this second Monday in October.
I lift my eyes to the eternal bay beyond,
and my gut hurts,
and I wonder what Penobscot men
would have thought
of conquering not for food
but for blood.

## The Plants of Acadia National Park

In the middle of January's blue caprice
(hey, it's the 15th already,
damn, it's only the 15th)
I pick up the book
and the plant names alone
transport me
(not to mention this marvel of publishing:
some five pounds of heavy glossy paper,
perfectly bound and trimmed,
with thousands of color pictures
of flowers, fruits, stems, leaves, trunks
often displayed against the bluest of summer skies).

First stop, Fun City Carnival:
Devil's Beggar-Tick, Low Cudweed, Mad-Dog Skullcap
Dragon's Mouth, Spreading Dogbane, Burning Bush

How about anatomy class:
Small Pussytoes, Dwarf Nipplewort,
Spotted Touch-Me-Not, Humped Bladderwort, Floating Heart, Whorled
Loosestrife, Swarthy Sedge, Starved Panic Grass, Naked Miterwort

Heaven, anyone?
Seaside Bluebell, Self-Heal, Sweet Everlasting
Live-Forever, Pearly Everlasting, Bliss

Winter's just fine if you've got
Acadia to drool over,
provided you skip the list
at the back of the book
(the 181 species not seen since 1980)
in favor of blessing the 862 still left.

## Barkskins

*For Annie Proulx*



                    Her
                  book is
                devastating:
              how we scraped
            the land; how everyone
          thought we were destined for
        greatness, or certainly wealth. It's
      impossible to read without grippe and
    ache. It was bad enough back then to hack
  trees down when they might still be considered
  a symbol tying heavens to earth, to a far God. It's
worse now. As we touch the bark, this skin between
blood and air, its rivers and grooves, its flows up and
down, they've become personal, our spirit plants
                    meaning
                    we need
                    no longer
                    indenture
                    ourselves
                    to a god -
            still
                  we
                        slash
                              trees
                                    down.

              Tell us then

        how             how         how
        many            hard        much
        we've           it is        we
        lost.           to root      share.
                         us
                         back
                         into
                         earth
                         unless

        we                              you.
            swing           among
              in hammocks

**March into April**

"I have an appointment with spring."

Google informs me
that none of the two million words
of Thoreau's Journal
offer any description, drawing,
or meticulous tracking of the emergence,
in spring, of the crocus.
Pity.
I would have liked to compare
his feelings with mine.
I would have liked to exceed his joy
in even one small way,
for if I plan it right,
I can meet spring's true and lovely sybil
not merely for a week
of walks between Walden and Concord
but for a month or more,
March and April, when
the distance between houses
of two hundred miles, not two,
makes a double spring. (Or prolongs winter.)
            ....

I also walk in the yarded, tended city
and I look intently for her spears
of purple, white, and yellow
pushing directly out of dirt
and stabbing the eye,
soft and hard at once.
Well, perhaps I have exceeded his joy.
He writes much of love, nothing of sex.
            ....
When I walk in Maine
he is at my side.
We don't find too many signs
of the strife among people.
Nor will we find crocus for a while.
There's not enough light and heat yet
to bud in her bed. Cold keeps her safe
until she's ready.

But she will arrive in April,
in the natural course of things.
            ....

For whatever reason
he could not (or was not allowed to)
find sexual love.
He did find love in general human kindness,
and of course, in chipmunks and perch,
orchids and trilliums.
Perhaps that's a better way to understand death.
            ...

But nature is changing now, unreliable.
Spring comes earlier and earlier.
Our flowers bloom several weeks ahead of his.
A quarter of the plants he recorded
have perished from the earth,
especially the cold-loving wildflowers.
And now the crocus too is rare,
lunch for the mice and chipmunks,
who, nearly tame, have colonized
our lawns and sit down with them like diners.
            ....

Plants in the northeast need winter,
a chilling period of rain and snow and ice,
as perhaps do I.
How many walks do I have left?
How many stabs of vigor?
Whence the thrill of emerging from February?
Will spring still "come to the window to wake me"
and climb into my bed?

## Whose Woods These Are

Warm light is dappling down, and moss
and ferns shine bright. I feel no loss
of darkened brush or tangled vine,
those deep and icy woods of Frost.

Whose woods these are I know. They're mine
and yours. Out front there is a sign
that says these lands are held in trust,
a human promise that's divine,

more prized than any Bible verse.
And so, Magog, parade your worst,
while for an hour we walk and smell
the trees - not tar, not car exhaust -

until we leave to drive pell-mell
through miles of Walmart, Ford, and Shell,
and pray the unborn will rebel
against such messengers from hell.

**Standing in Woods on a Fall Morning**

Silence for a spell.
No breeze
through the tops of the trees.
No promises to fill.

As leaves twirl and fall
I can hear them
(no, you can't).

They sound when they land
(whisper of winter),
and a downy breeze above
sends down more dancers,
sends down more dancers.

# The Edge of the Ledge

**Green Man**

Another oak has fallen on the shore.
There he lies, beside his brothers,
splayed on beds of gravel, rockweed,
boulders, sand,
and a great new hole is torn
in the bank above,
of shifting, friable, glacial moraine.

Through three-score years of questing,
I have looked to trees for strength,
above all
this particular glorious line
of fathers, pagans, spirits,
whose green and noble heads
sway with tales of death and birth.

He's fallen yet will live.
For high tides lap
his bits of limb and leaf,
skin and heart,
into the forever sea —
I wish he could have walked,
and I be rooted.

# In Midair

my view of the bay is narrow
but deep
ash trees on one side   ↓   oaks on the other
↓
↓
a cleft into the next world

the horizon slips
and blues merge
(water island hill cloud shadow)
beckoning

midair
an osprey
spotlit in the setting sun
nearly still against the changing winds
hangs between heaven and earth
tells shadow from fish
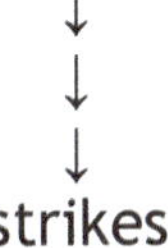
strikes

**Erosion**

The bank at ocean's edge is crumbling fast.
Leaning for years, the oak tree finally falls.
Leaves can't breathe and break apart in salt.

Life's stress and booze and drugs have made a mess
of our mucosal cells. We have clutched
our guts in pain. Order turns to mush.

The spirits of the Whites corrode the weald
and confidence of Native sovereignty.
Once-proud tribes must battle entropy.

What chance have Earth's most intricate of schemes
against Deere or Caterpillar steel?
Mayhem's ultimate ally is greed.

The universe is bent to decompose,
unless we energize our moral souls.

## Cash on the Bank

In order to help hit the price
he pulls from the air,
the realtor suggests
we gin up the view
by hacking down bushes,
and "raising the canopy"
of the oaks on the shore.

OK, true,
though we can't help but feel
that trimming a tree
is a step too far,
very unlike
grooming a poodle for show,
rouging a cheek for profit,
and all manner of things
that humans do to impress,
which is worth how much again?

**Surf**

At the end of my life
someone book me a flight
on time's wingèd wheelchair.
Land me here
on the edge
of the ledge,
let me finish my rest
in your restlessness.

## Stabilization

If I had a little playfulness
and lots of imagination today
the excavators on the shore over there
might be herons stabbing at fish.

But in this foul fog of a mood
imagination travels nowhere near
any country of play.
Riprap is being laid
to armor the land,
and the blaring bang of steel against rock
announces rumors and portents:
The glaciers are melting,
storms flooding,
and giant surf will break up these bluffs.

Out in the bay the barge and the tug
await high tide.
They gather the herons
to safety,
push off towards the horizon,
leave this bolus of chopped-up granite
to fight the sea-fevers fueled
by dead zooplankton.

Yet the moods of the sea,
the hot acid monsters of it,
the very things that threaten us,
are the only prescription
that calms me now.

Its deep-seated patience
and playful facade
shore up my hopes
for stabilization.

## A Heron Flies Low

What is more romantic
than Adirondacks on a lawn,
weathered and gray,
angled toward each other,
arms touching,
facing the bay.

Two doves perch,
one on each chair.
Alone, on the deck above,
I listen to them coo.

A heron flies low,
away to misty islands.

# The Sea Pulses

## For Love of the Sea

This far north on Penobscot Bay, ennobling surf is rare.
But winds weave wave patterns worthy of kings' robes.

Amazing grace of a February morning at twelve below:
Sea smoke marching across the bay like spirits to glory.

As if the parades of mighty surf were not enough to lift
me up, its sound - abyssal, cloacal - dissolves my mind.

Bands of blue, orange, violet, red sliding from the west
across the gulf re-pink the granite on Schoodic's shore.

Below: orca, octopus, kraken, shark, moray, leviathans.
Above: duck, heron, eagle, gull, osprey, loon, seraphim.

The number of times I've sailed on the sea is wickedly
slim - another awkward instance of looking, not doing.

The immensity of what is seen and what stays obscure
makes me feel safe. A humble man won't feel exposed.

**End of the Season**

The boats patrol before dawn,
a pair of them stalking
small schools of pogies,
which are, you appreciate,
a crucial fish in the sea
for filtering our bays when they feed,
for offering their flesh
to fish and birds innumerable,
and now being asked to sacrifice
more.

The State has ended the season early this year,
as one more tragedy of the commons appears.
Hacked into chunks of flesh for lobster bait,
fish end as chunks of flab on tourist shanks,
and pad the accounts of
      wholesalers
         packagers
            forwarders
               retailers
                  restaurateurs -

let me here interrupt this sermon with another
and say that at this season of life,
I'd rather be taken by
talon or tooth
than by nets of nylon,
be slain by nature than by vertical markets.

I'd rather be shortening the links
in the great chain of eating,
and offer my flesh to the worms of green burial,
than padding the accounts of the funeral conglomerate -

amen, and praise be to all creatures here below.

## A Small River Meets a Huge Sea

If his life will be caught in a fantasy,
it might not be fair
for a boy on puberty's edge
to be set free on this half mile of sand,
which will take all afternoon to explore
since he's never seen the ocean before.

To the north, the ruins of a fort
built to help keep the Union.
Just offshore an island he can reach,
he's told, at low tide, later.
A few shelves of granite
draped in fresh seaweed.
Broken crab shells.
His family,
Midwest visiting East,
eating baloney sandwiches,
huddling together on blankets.
Gulls waiting.
Staffs of ancient music written in sand.

Then he's off,
to the south end of the beach
where the river comes out,
where fresh and saltwater mix,
where timid trout stop,
sensing sharks,
where a pine-covered hill
and a yet wilder beach,
untrammeled, driftwood in chaos,
beckon just a few yards away.

But this side is enough for today,
for he has now known a place
where prospects seem endless.
The sea pulses. The horizon shimmers.
Something held down breaks open.
He is embraced.

# Sea Smoke

Cold hands in the air
touch the warm heart of the sea
Sea smoke on the bay

There's something out there
Let's bark at it like crazy
Sea smoke on the bay

The Internet thinks
faster than we do, fogs brains
Sea smoke on the bay

It takes zero or
less to waken the spirits
Sea smoke on the bay

Clouds move like angels
guarding our near-by heaven
Sea smoke on the bay

**Riding It Out**

The sheltered cove is skimmed with ice,
and newscasts call for sacrifice.

Yet skeins of scoters land and strive
to break the jam, to dab and dive,
to band together to survive
the first cold day of dire '25.

# Burning Up the Sky

## All Rivers Lead to the Sea

From my little perch the ocean looks healthy,
thrilling and calming,
but the Anthropocene forces a view
beyond the armchair, deeper than skin.

Ubiquitous amorous ships kiss the waves.
Below, the blast of their engines
deafens dolphins,
makes humpbacks bleed,
kills krill.
Garbage from storm drains
floats in patches
twice the size of Texas.
Microplastics flow down,
rain down,
wreak God knows what damage
on the organs of fish.
Carbon thrusts in,
acids assault, dissolve
a crab's carapace.
Minerals leak from farms and lawns.
They grow life on the land,
they deal death in the water.

Everything ends in the sea,
and the rivers run like tears of salt
down the beautiful face
of a woman abused.

**Sounds Off**

I might mistake
the roar of trucks on US 1
for wind in oaks
if I snap off my resentments for a while
and watch the flock of gulls
circling above the bay
flashing white in the sun
like rippling roulades in Chopin.

       In that moment
       my inside is outside

until a klutzy quacking troop of ducks
flying up from ocean's stage
bombs about as if annoyed
heads north to another hermit's cove
ends my perfect deafness.

Edges form again.

Traffic is a sempiternal groan again
and I too head north
to headphones
("Nocturne Opus 9, Number 1," Claudio Arrau)

thus, to mitigate
the shameful contracts humans make
requiring Camembert and Lindt
to be on hand at every Stop & Shop
just up the road.

## Rovers Take Pictures on Mars

Five hundred years ago,
corporate white men
in ships grandly named —
*Santa Maria, Ark Royal, Gift of God* —
sailed to new worlds
and wrote glowing accounts
of wealth to be won.
These days
rovers looking cutely like humans
crawl in Mars dust,
and for the amazement of Earthlings
post photos of ore
on their first-person
Twitter accounts.
The names haven't changed all that much —
*Sojourner, Spirit, Opportunity, Perseverance* —
absent the presence of God
and red men to tame.
Now, move forward another five centuries:
anonymous near-human robots
sail from Billionaires' Bubble
to the asteroid belt,
mining it
out.

# Product

*for Bill McKibben*

The word was invented
when English was young:
from *productum*, Latin, something brought forth,
merely meaning, then, the result of x times y,
until the nineteenth century, full of iron,
disfigured life, nature, language altogether,
hard and brutally, but not yet ironically,
which the twenty-first neatly takes care of,
as vast wealthy hordes of us leave our fruitful careers,
but not our cultural training in being productive.
    (can't just rest, you know, must do stuff)
        gardens, libraries, pools  →
            the accouterments of castles
        pickleball, golf, regattas  →
            the proxies of one-upmanship
        travel, shopping, dining  →
            the mementos of consumption
        painting, pottery, poetry  →
            the redemptions of capitalism
        charity, boards, memoir  →
            the canonizations of birthright

One poor Dutch-American schmuck (me)
reviewing his output at age seventy-two,
still blames the Father (John Calvin)
who said, on his deathbed,
"What! Would you have the Lord find me idle when He comes?"

Yes! (I wish?) At least take a moment,
for (let me break it gently to you all)
the dark Lord is already burning up the sky,
and even the civilized things you plan to do
further consume Our Earth.

Breathe in now while we can.

Remember the Proto-Indo-European root -
*per*, forward, *deuk*, to lead -
and get out our checkbooks,
fill up our calendars,
and re-write Act Three
of the coming catastrophe.

## Better

Navigate the slope.
Clear the path of vine and roots,
wield the pruner pole.
Lop the ragged shoots
and throw them down the bank.
Regain the deck,
enjoy a bigger, better view of bay,
nature now in check.

Just hack a bush
or two…. not about
to dam a river, pave a marsh,
mine a mountain, scoop a pit,
nowhere near that harsh,
right?

## Earthrise

What a rush and a startle
to set out to circle the moon,
and discover the Earth instead,
to be little Apollos in titanium tubes,
our vivid blue marble in view,
half cat's eye, half purie,
and the warm scarf of air that surrounds it
so thin, like a skin of plastic
wrapped round a ball.

Space may be God,
but where are the balsams,
sunrise, borealis, and eagles,
lovers on moss beds,
alewives in streams?
And space has no delirious up or
grounding of down,
just a constant, barren, circling
around.

Fifty years later,
here are my wishes:
that ten thousand satellites
now junking the sky
might flame out like meteors;
that rocket man billionaires
lusting for Mars
find some other phallus to finger;
that Earth be restored —

Focus the Hubble on us.

**Cruisers**

Two cheetahs
chase down an antelope,
eat —
in seconds boxes of steel
breathing exhaust
surround them,
like lookers-on
in *Boogie Nights*.

We amber the cats in silicon and glass,
cruise back to glam camp,
bask —
and fly home to safety in tubes of aluminum,
to show off our trophies,
resume consuming.

Land Cruisers get junked on the veldt,
Galaxies leak in landfills,
Dreamliners rust in the desert,
but skin, haunch, guts live again,
even bone re-absorbed —
nothing is wasted in nature.

**Insectageddon**

Like the gases you spew, you'd rather not see us.
You ignore us, in fact,
and when we do emerge in your snug, smug world,
you get righteous and squeamish and scared.
We include dung beetles, locusts, honeybees, mosquitoes.
On the one hand, we amass, and we ruin your fields and your health.
On the other, we are rapidly dying - and so will most flowers and birds.
We outnumber you, a hundred-and-twenty-five million to one,
we even outweigh you, seventeen to one,
yet it's you who are upending the balance of life.
We service the Earth.
You flee into space, lusting for minerals on moons.

## The Moon Moves

If I sit perfectly still for a while,
I can watch the moon
move up the sky,
one bare oak branch, then another,
slicing across its full yellow rind
until it's eaten by clouds...
and then the ersatz candescence
of the port at Mack Point,
its spot-lighted tanks full of propane and poisons,
usurps the view in the usual way.

Time to blur again unblinkered eyes:
imagine the absence of tankers,
believe that the moon makes its own pagan light,
and celebrate time to spend musing,
imperfectly wild in the dark.

## What Kind of Man

sees an oak and thinks board feet,
sees a stream and thinks a dam,
sees a meadow and thinks a mall,
sees the sky and thinks a plane?

The civilized kind, I am afraid,
in times that need guerillas.

# Sit Here a While

## Birds (Praying)

One lone mourning dove
perches on the dead, topmost
branch of an ash tree,

cooing. Only males
coo, I know, and his aim
is not one of mourning -

still: my aunt has been left
widowed in their homestead
of sixty-some years,

and we've just come back
from burying John's ashes
in a hole in the woods,

and I can do nothing
but sit here a while, wishing
for simpler things,

while around my feeder,
hummingbirds war,
bills clacking like rosaries,

and overhead
an airplane bows to the sun,
droning sutras and smoke,

and crows on the shore
make orisons loud enough
to raise up the dead.

**Through a Glass**

I look up to see,
on the other side of the window,
bare trees, a calm sea.
The glass is clear.
Is that a lynx in the snow?
For a moment I see as a child might see.

What's that feeling
when you behold a wonder
and fall far short in describing it —
impotence by reason of self-consciousness?
For I have typed "Nature is"
and the glass became a clouded mirror
holding a dark face.

It's seldom that words
slip perfectly into place.
The likes of "friend" and "fox" and "freeze"
come close,
but then we do that big and clumsy human thing,
try to name abstractions,
and the self barges in,
blinding us for a while, sans links,
in no man's land.

St. Paul was blinded too —
in a vision of God, he claimed —
and finally gave up on life:
"For now, we see through a glass, darkly.
But then face to face."

I almost never agree
with one of history's great hypocrites,
but intimacy does heal denatured souls,
just not where — sitting in sancta,
or in some gilted heaven —
such saints expect it,
Go through the glass
into a limpid river pool
or a loving close embrace
and stay there wordlessly,
for more than a moment.

**Quarks**

*For GFL*

A poet I know lives on Noyes Street.          
Not Dogma Drive
where what we see
is what we get,
but a neighborhood of wavicles, oscillations, uncertainties,
where houses only tend to exist,
where a hockey puck rippling a backyard net
only tends to occur....
So, solid things might not be.
Guts and wheelbarrows
comprise quarks colliding and bosons spinning,
un-pin-down-able.
It's not a contradiction,
that home both entangles and frees,
that courage cannot exist without fear,
that grief is a torso muscled in emptiness.
These are polarities,
electric,
the ends of an oval,
and we are sparks fleetingly etched
in an orbit often too beautiful
for words.

**So Beautiful Today**

Try to understand, She says,
why I must be
so beautiful today.

You should bathe
in bits of sky and sea,
breathe in my Earthly air.
Believe in what I am
and don't obsess on stars,
or fugues of feats long past.
Don't quarrel with the fog and cold to come,
and if you ask me why,
you'll get your boxers in a bunch,
for I'll persist,
and you will not,
making "why" both brave
and risible.

**End Times**

A young-aged man,
living on hope, dreams of rivers —
creeks that flee the theistic plains,
brooks running hand-in-hand with trout
through well-watered woods —
but not of deltas and mouths,
and the great dirty cities
like the one in which he must toil,
muddying the waters.
Time is an ever-rolling stream.
He never needs step
in the same hole twice.

A middle-aged man,
striving too hard in the suburbs,
gets to spend time with his family
on a well-cottaged shore.
He is seduced by the tides,
for the sea is a twice-a-day lover,
bedding and baring the land,
loyal when others are not.
Sometimes he goes off alone,
and yet he is not,
for he mixes his metaphors
(at the end will mix molecules)
with ospreys exploding at high tide
and herons brooding at low.
Time doesn't run there,
it mostly sloshes back and forth.

An old-aged man,
seeing at last that time will dry up,
postpones the dream
of a permanent perch on a hermit's wild ledge.
He needs a few friends, he's found,
and isn't he privileged
to live in two kinds of 'burbs
(one at least on the flight path of eagles,
one that is stippled with human affection),
and to worry hardly at all, for now,
what end times might herald:
archangel or starlight,
right choice or wrong,
all or nothing.

## Morning, Late February

The sun is still low in the southeastern sky,
but slipping through ash trees an omen of May
alights on my pale winter face like a flame.

        Remain still.

Don't think it, don't mull it, don't chew it, don't try

        to foretell

the snow that will fall by the end of the day,
the doom of the carbon engulfing our realm,
the house on a ledge by the sea in my dream.

Remember that we get our manna of joy
administered only in crumbs, out of time.

**Buzzed**

Ah, to make thinking a muddle
and feelings a knife….
Because you're sitting outside,
you've poured that second elixir,
silvery, tinkly,
closing in
on earth's high tremors.
You sail for a while
over the bay, with the rioting crows,
then happily, tipsily, sink
to earth's low terrors,
to the worm or the claw,
where it's clearer
that every death, little and big,
gives life,
sometimes quickly
(osprey, mackerel, chick),
or in a while
(you, casket, maggots).

So, here's to a third,
to a nice naked rot in the dirt,
and a dramatic rebirth,
say, as a mushroom that sprouts overnight,
erect, ever-hopeful,
thick with serum and sinew.

## Love Song

I see that three juvenile loons
have chosen this stretch of shore
on the coast of Maine
to spend their winter
wailing love songs
to future mates
on summer ponds,
like teenage boys
their voices breaking,
as mine does
when I go backwards
from the age of 75 to then,
not to mention going
sideways, now,
to you.

## Acknowledgments

Thanks to the following publications for first appearance of these poems.

"Multitudes" - *Arc Poetry* Vol. 99, October 2022
"Bird Baiting" - Portland Press Herald *Deep Water* poems, September 3, 2023
"He and She" - *Uppagus* Vol. 62, May 2024
"Overnight Success" - *Wayfarer*, August 2025
"Red or Blue" - *Portrait of New England* Vol. 7, July 2025
"Cabbage White" - *The Northeast Coast* Vol I, May 2025
"White Man's Footstep" - *The Fourth River (Tributaries)*, December 2023
"Turkeys" - *The River*, October 2024
"Barkskins" - *The River*, October 2024
"March into April" - *Spire*, April 2023
"Whose Woods These Are" - *Orchards Poetry Journal*, July 2024
"Standing in Woods on a Fall Morning" - *Livina Press*, February 2025
"Green Man" - *Grey Sparrow* Vol. 45, January 2025
"A Heron Flies Low" - *North Dakota Quarterly* 92:1/2, July 2025
"For Love of the Sea" - *Spillwords*, September 2022
"End of the Season" - *Sage*, April 2025
"Rovers Take Pictures on Mars" - *Nine Muses* Vol. III, January 2025
"Product" - *Spire*, April 2023
"Earthrise" - *Ionosphere* - January 2026
"Insectageddon" - *Poets for Science*, November 2024
"The Moon Moves" - *Comstock Review* 37:2, February 2024
"Birds (Praying)" - *Slippery Elm 2025*, November 2025
"Quarks" - *Euphony* 25:1, March 2025
"Morning Late February" - *Panoply* Vol. 23, January 2023
"Love Song" - *Northern New England Review* Vol. 43, March 2024

# About the Author

Jim Krosschell has published poems and essays in some 85 journals, plus two essay collections: *One Man's Maine*, which won a Maine Literary Award, and *Owls Head Revisited*. He lives in Deer Isle, ME and Newton, MA, and volunteers on Boards for Coastal Mountains Land Trust and the Maine Writers & Publishers Alliance.

www.ingramcontent.com/pod-product-compliance
Lightning Source LLC
Chambersburg PA
CBHW080340030726
47594CB00012B/4090